D1402758

How People Lived in America
Keeping in Touch in American History

by Dana Meachen Rau

Reading consultant:
Susan Nations, M.Ed.,
author/literacy coach/
consultant in literacy development

Please visit our web site at: www.garethstevens.com
For a free color catalog describing Weekly Reader® Early Learning Library's list
of high-quality books, call 1-877-445-5824 (USA) or 1-800-387-3178 (Canada).
Weekly Reader® Early Learning Library's fax: (414) 336-0164.

Library of Congress Cataloging-in-Publication Data

Rau, Dana Meachen, 1971-
    Keeping in touch in American history / by Dana Meachen Rau.
       p. cm. — (How people lived in America)
    Includes bibliographical references and index.
    ISBN-10: 0-8368-7208-8 — ISBN-13: 978-0-8368-7208-8 (lib. bdg.)
    ISBN-10: 0-8368-7215-0 — ISBN-13: 978-0-8368-7215-6 (softcover)
    1. Communication—United States—History. I. Title.
  P92.U5R38 2007
  302.20973—dc22   2006008630

This edition first published in 2007 by
Weekly Reader® Early Learning Library
A Member of the WRC Media Family of Companies
330 West Olive Street, Suite 100
Milwaukee, WI 53212 USA

Editor: Barbara Kiely Miller
Art direction: Tammy West
Cover design and page layout: Kami Strunsee
Picture research: Sabrina Crewe

Picture credits: Cover, title page, p. 19 © Bettmann/CORBIS; p. 4 © Michael Newman/
PhotoEdit; pp. 6, 8, 9, 10, 11, 13, 14, 15, 16, 17 © North Wind Picture Archives; p. 7
© Lowell Georgia/CORBIS; pp. 12, 20 The Granger Collection, New York; p. 18
© Underwood & Underwood/CORBIS; p. 21 © Bob Daemmrich/PhotoEdit

Printed in the United States of America

1 2 3 4 5 6 7 8 9 10 09 08 07 06

Table of Contents

Cover: Early telephones were large and hung on the wall. When people talked on the telephone, they had to stand very close to it.

Children use computers in school and at home to keep in touch.

Keeping in Touch Today

Today, sending an **e-mail** to a friend is a fast and easy way to keep in touch. But long ago, people could not send messages quickly. People had to wait days, months, or years for news from someone who lived far away.

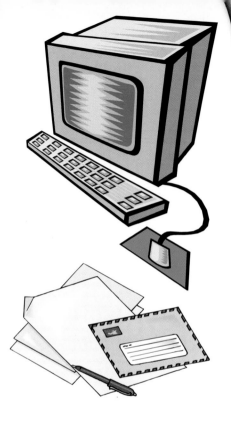

Long ago, people . . .

- ✏ did not write with pens and pencils;
- ✏ did not talk to people far away;
- ✏ did not have radios or televisions;
- ✏ did not have cell phones;
- ✏ did not have email or computers;
- ✏ did not have text messaging.

News Travels Slowly

Writing with a quill pen took a long time. People had time to think about what they wanted to write.

In the 1600s, many **settlers** in America lived far apart. They wrote letters to each other to share news. People wrote with **quill pens** made from long feathers. A writer dipped the point of a quill into a pot of ink. The empty space inside the quill filled with ink. The person could write a few words. Then the quill had to be filled up again.

People **sealed,** or closed, their letters with melted wax. They gave their letters to travelers passing through town. They might even pay the travelers to carry the letters. A letter sent this way might not arrive for months. If the wax seal was broken, the person getting the letter knew someone else had read it.

A seal was carved with a name or initials. The seal was pressed into melted wax to help close a letter and show who wrote it.

Paul Revere rode through towns to bring important news. He spread news of people fighting for freedom.

In 1711, a **postal** system made sending and getting mail easier. Men rode horses from town to town to deliver letters. People built post roads between cities so the riders could carry the mail quickly. People in town picked up their mail at the post office or a local **inn**.

Reading the News

People read news in newspapers, too. People called **printers** made newspapers on a **printing press**. Early newspapers were only four pages long. They came out once a week. Newspapers had news from England. They also had stories about the government, fires, and items for sale.

© North Wind Picture Archives

This is a picture of the first printing press in America. It could print only one newspaper at a time.

Poor Richard, 1733.

AN

Almanack

For the Year of Chrift

1733,

Being the Firft after LEAP YEAR:

And makes fince the Creation	Years
By the Account of the Eaftern *Greeks*	7241
By the Latin Church, when ☉ ent. ♈	6932
By the Computation of *W. W*	5742
By the *Roman* CHronology	5682
By the *Jewifh* Rabbies	5494

Wherein is contained

The Lunations, Eclipfes, Judgment of the Weather, Spring Tides, Planets Motions & mutual Afpects, Sun and Moon's Rifing and Setting, Length of Days, Time of High Water, Fairs, Courts, and obfervable Days

Fitted to the Latitude of Forty Degrees, and a Meridian of Five Hours Weft from *London*, but may without fenfible Error, ferve all the adjacent Places, even from *Newfoundland* to *South-Carolina.*

By *RICHARD SAUNDERS*, Philom.

PHILADELPHIA:

Printed and fold by *B. FRANKLIN*, at the New Printing Office near the Market.

The Third Impreffion.

Printers made **almanacs**, too. Almanacs were small books used by farmers, fishermen, and others. They included calendars, weather reports, and tips on planting crops. Some almanacs had news and short stories.

Poor Richard's Almanac was written and printed by Benjamin Franklin. He was a famous inventor.

Some towns did not have printers. The people in these towns heard the news from a town **crier**. He rang a bell to get the attention of the townspeople. Then he shouted, or cried out, the news. He announced when a ship was coming in or other important news.

Town criers helped lost children find their parents.

People were excited when a stagecoach pulled into town.
It brought mail and people from other places.

Speedy Messages

In the 1800s, more people moved to lands and towns in
the West. **Stagecoaches** brought mail on the long trip
west. Railroads began crossing America, too. Trains
could carry heavy loads of mail, but the trip still took
a long time.

Some people who had to send a message quickly used the **Pony Express**. This was a mail route that ran from Missouri to California. A horseback rider carried a mailbag. He rode as fast as he could from station to station. He switched horses often so they did not get too tired. Every 100 miles (160 kilometers), the riders changed. A new rider took the mailbag and continued the trip.

A Pony Express rider did not stay at a station very long. He quickly jumped off his tired horse and onto a fresh one. Then he was back on the trail again!

© North Wind Picture Archives

© North Wind Picture Archives

The young Pony Express riders had to keep going through bad snowstorms and rain. The youngest rider was only eleven years old!

Pony Express riders had to be small so the horses could run fast. Only boys younger than eighteen were hired. In just ten days, these young men could cover almost 2,000 miles (3,218 km). But the Pony Express lasted only from 1860 to 1861. Another invention made sending messages even faster.

Samuel Morse invented the **telegraph** in 1837. The telegraph was a machine that sent messages through wires. A set of long or short taps stood for each letter in the alphabet. The person sending the message tapped the code for each letter of a message into the telegraph. Each tap sent an electric signal.

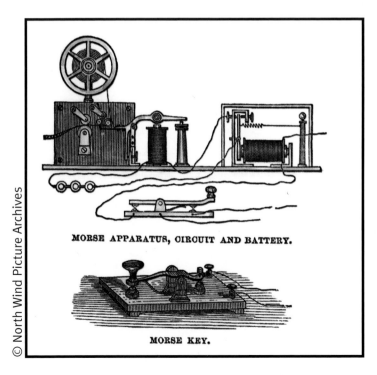

MORSE APPARATUS, CIRCUIT AND BATTERY.

MORSE KEY.

The system of taps used with a telegraph was called Morse code. The code was tapped in using the machine's key.

The **signals** traveled in the wires that hung between towns and cities. A telegraph machine at the other end received the signals. An arm on the machine tapped out the code onto a strip of paper. Someone who knew the code wrote out the message. The message was given or taken to the person it was for. At last, people could get news right after it happened!

Telegraph wires were often strung on poles put up next to train tracks.

Alexander Graham Bell wondered if voices could be sent through wires, too. In 1876, he created the telephone. People who were miles apart could now talk to each other using telephones. An **operator** connected the person making a call to the person being called.

Alexander Graham Bell is shown making the first call from New York to Chicago. Early telephones were called "speaking telegraphs."

These boys were at camp in 1929. They gathered to listen to the latest news on the radio each night.

News in the Air

At the end of the 1800s, some people discovered that they did not need wires to send signals. Radios could send signals through the air. At first, radio stations sent out codes, as telegraphs had. Stations soon started sending voices and music through the air. Tall **antennas** sent out the signals. Other antennas picked up the sounds.

Signals for pictures could be sent through the air, too. Television shows were made and sent out by TV stations. By the 1950s, many homes had TVs. Families watched news shows. They heard important speeches. They learned what the weather was going to be like the next day. People learned about life in the rest of the country and the world.

This family watched the president of the United States on TV. Their daughter was on the program with him!

This computer from the 1940s was one of the first large computers made. Today, computers are much faster and can do more work.

Computers gave people a new way to keep in touch. In the 1940s, the first computers were as big as a room. In the 1970s, people could buy smaller computers to use at work and at home. In the 1980s, people started using computers to send messages. An e-mail is a message sent from one computer to another.

Long ago, messages took months to travel from person to person. Today, people still send letters and read newspapers, just as they did years ago. But people can also receive messages seconds after they are sent. Thanks to computers, we are still finding new ways to keep in touch.

These women read a text message sent to them on a cell phone.

Glossary

almanacs — books that come out once a year containing a calendar, numerical facts, and information on many subjects

antennas — the parts used to send or receive radio waves

e-mail — a message sent from one computer to another, it stands for electronic mail

inn — a place that has meals and rooms for travelers

operator — a person who operates, or runs, a machine. A telephone operator connects calls from different phone lines.

postal — having to do with mail

printers — people who make copies of newspapers, books, or other things to read

printing press — a machine that presses paper against an inked surface to make copies

quill pens — writing tools made from bird feathers

settlers — people who move to and develop a new area

signals — tiny pieces of information that travel through wires or air

stagecoaches — horse-drawn coaches with four wheels that carried passengers and mail

For More Information

Books

I Wonder Why the Telephone Rings and Other Questions About Communication. I Wonder Why (series). Richard Mead (Kingfisher)

They're Off!: The Story of the Pony Express. Cheryl Harness (Aladdin)

Where Does the Mail Go?: A Book About the Postal System. Discovery Readers (series). Melvin and Gilda Berger (Chelsea House Publications)

Web Site

The Franklin Institute Online
sln.fi.edu/franklin/
Facts about Benjamin Franklin and other inventors

Publisher's note to educators and parents: Our editors have carefully reviewed this Web site to ensure that it is suitable for children. Many Web sites change frequently, however, and we cannot guarantee that a site's future contents will continue to meet our high standards of quality and educational value. Be advised that children should be closely supervised whenever they access the Internet.

Index

About the Author

Dana Meachen Rau is the author of more than one hundred and fifty children's books, including nonfiction and books for early readers. She writes about history, science, geography, people, and even toys! She lives with her family in Burlington, Connecticut.